JAMESTOWN PUBLISHERS

THE CONTEMPORARY READER

VOLUME 1, NUMBER 6

CONTENTS

4 SETTING THE SKY ON FIRE
What's behind a great show of fireworks?

14 FAITH, FAMILY, AND FARMING
What can we learn from the Amish people? Can their way of life survive in the modern world?

26 FIDDLER WITH A SMILE
How did a boy who was seriously disabled become a world-famous violinist?

36 STAIRWAYS TO HEAVEN
In which lands are some of the world's most beautiful churches? Why were these huge structures built?

48 CAN THE DEAD TALK?
How did a Chicago stabbing victim help solve her own murder?

56

THE TRUE WORLD CHAMPIONSHIP
Why is soccer the most popular game in the world?

66

A MAN WITH A VISION
Can one person make a difference? What is special about a man who put his country first?

76

THE DIFFERENCE A DAY MAKES
Why was there no October 5 in the year 1582?

86

A NEW KIND OF COMPANY
Can a company make a lot of money and do good at the same time?

What's behind a great show of fireworks?

SETTING THE SKY ON FIRE

1 The night explodes in color and light. Streaks of red, white, and gold flash across the sky. A huge boom comes with it. A crowd watches from the ground. Sounds of "oooh" and "aaah" can be heard along with claps and cheers.

2   Almost everyone enjoys watching fireworks. What would Fourth of July celebrations be without them?

HISTORY

3   The Chinese sent up fireworks more than 1,000 years ago. That tells us the Chinese knew how to use the black powder that goes into making fireworks. Gunpowder is made from black powder, too. But gunpowder wasn't used until the invention of the first muskets[1] and cannons in the 1300s. So we know that people used black powder for fun long before they used it to kill.

4   Word of fireworks spread from China into Europe during the Middle Ages. An English monk, Roger Bacon, wrote about making fireworks in 1242. However, Bacon thought they were so dangerous that he wrote the instructions in secret code.

BLACK MAGIC

5   Making the black powder that goes into fireworks hasn't changed much over time. It is 75 parts saltpeter, 15 parts charcoal, and 10 parts sulfur. All it takes is a spark or fuse to set

---

[1] muskets: heavy guns used before modern rifles

Sparks fly in sharp contrast to the calm of this beach at sunset.

it off. The mixture burns fast. Gases given off by the fire gush into the air and cause a blast.

6   Setting off black powder makes a bright light. The light itself won't have any color, though. Color is determined by the length of the light rays. To make the different rays, certain metal salts are added to the fireworks. Sodium makes a yellow-orange color. Strontium [stron'•she•uhm] makes red. Copper makes blue and barium green. When you add magnesium [mag•nee'•zee•uhm] and aluminum powder, it makes the colors glow. Now you know why fireworks are called "chemistry dressed up in flashy clothing."

7   A really rich blue flame is the hardest to make. A blue flame calls for copper chloride, which won't work if it gets too hot. Getting the blue just right is an art. Purple isn't easy to make either, because the rays for that color are the shortest. So when you see good blue or purple fireworks, you know that the fireworks artists are experts.

Blasts of light, color, and sound thrill crowds at the Louvre Museum of Art in Paris, France.

SHELL SHOCK

8 Fireworks zoom into the air as shells packed in tubes. Most makers of American and European fireworks use a ball-shaped shell. Lighting the black powder at the bottom of the shell sends it into the air. At the same time, a fuse lights. Once in the air, the fuse goes off and breaks open the shell. The hot gases push out the "stars," sending a shower of light and color into the sky. The "boom" sound comes a few seconds later because sound doesn't travel as fast as light.

9   One kind of shell, called a *salute*, makes only a flash of light and a loud boom. Other shells contain more than one part. As each part goes off, it lights the next part, which creates one burst after another in the sky.

All Shapes and Sizes

10   Have you ever seen fireworks in a pinwheel shape? That shape starts as a long paper tube rolled up tight. Once in the air, the stars pop from the shell and spin in fancy shapes. The way the shell is packed into the tube determines the shape of fireworks. The Japanese kind of shell also sends up a shell in a tube. In this case, the black powder lies in the center of the ball, not at the bottom. This sets off the stars in a round, even shape. It may even set off a trail of light. And if there is more than one color chemical in the shell, the trail will change colors as it goes off.

Family Secrets

11   The secrets of making fireworks have been well kept over the years. Families have passed down information to their children, their children's children, and so on. Even today, most of the

Creative designs, like these pencils of light, are the work of a true fireworks artist.

world's great fireworks are made by just a few family businesses.

12   The famous fireworks families in the United States are the Gruccis of New York, the Zambellis of Pennsylvania, the Rozzis of Ohio, and the Souzas of California. Only in recent years have fireworks been studied much outside of these families. These studies have helped make fireworks more dazzling, more colorful, and even safer.

BEING CAREFUL

13 Safety remains a problem, though, in the care and handling of fireworks. Even small ones can be quite dangerous if they're used carelessly.

The Oakland Bay Bridge in San Francisco heightens the effect of this dazzling display of fireworks.

After every Fourth of July, there are new tragic stories about fireworks usage gone wrong. That is why the laws are tough when it comes to selling and handling fireworks.

14   Owners of fireworks firms work hard at being careful. One spark in a fireworks plant can blow everything up. In one plant, workers must touch a copper plate as they enter. This removes any electrical charge from a person's body. Inside, workers take care not to rub against each other. And they wouldn't even think of lighting a match!

15   In 1983, one spark set an entire plant on fire, killing two people. Since the accident, the plant owners purchase shells from smaller companies. That way, the most dangerous work is already done.

Enjoy the Show

16 Should just anyone try making fireworks? Of course not. Most of us should not even try to set off the kinds of fireworks available for purchase. Even a simple sparkler gets hot enough to burn a person very badly. The work of setting the sky on fire is best left to trained professionals. We have only to sit back and enjoy the show. ♦

Questions

1. How many years ago did the Chinese use fireworks?

2. What makes the color in fireworks?

3. Which colors are the hardest to make?

4. Why does the sound of the blast come after the light?

5. Why are there strong laws about selling and using fireworks?

*What can we learn from the Amish people?
Can their way of life survive in
the modern world?*

Faith,
Family,
and
Farming

**Amish travel by horse and buggy, which can pose
problems in heavy traffic.**

1   The Amish people of Lancaster County, Pennsylvania, share a 300-year-old tradition. Their society is based on faith, family, and farming. Every part of their life, from clothes to work, is part of their faith. And living in our modern world isn't easy.

THEIR HISTORY

2   The ancestors[1] of the Amish belonged to the Swiss Anabaptist religion. They believed in adult, not infant, baptism. In the 1600s, this belief caused punishment by death in many European countries. To avoid persecution,[2] many Anabaptists moved to farms. They wanted to be self-sufficient[3] [suh•fish'•ent]. They worshiped in private homes, not public churches.

3   Jacob Ammann was a church leader who wanted to make some changes. In 1693, he and his followers split from the Anabaptists. They became known as the *Amish.*

4   In the mid-1700s, to escape persecution, the Amish came to America. Here, some of them

---

[1] ancestors: relatives more distant than grandparents
[2] persecution: the act of causing someone to suffer because of belief
[3] self-sufficient: able to take care of oneself without outside help

changed their beliefs. They broke away to start their own sects.[4] Today, Amish live in 22 states and in Canada. The Lancaster County group is the oldest Amish settlement in the world.

5   The Old Order Amish here are the most traditional. Their clothing has hardly changed since Jacob Ammann's time. They use horses to farm and horse-drawn buggies for travel. They still worship in private homes.

THE FARMS

6   The average Amish farm is 60 acres. This is small enough to farm with a team of horses or mules. But it requires the whole family to work on it. Milk is a main product. Almost all families have a herd of about 50 cows. Farming teaches the children the values of their parents and the importance of hard work.

7   The average Amish family has seven children. When a son marries, his father gives him his own farm. Late autumn is wedding time in Lancaster. Almost 200 couples marry every year, and each couple would prefer to have their own farm. But a farmer can divide his farm only so many times.

---

[4] sects: religious groups having beliefs that differ greatly from those of the main body

The Amish believe that a farm is the best place to raise children.

8   Lancaster County has excellent farmland. It's close to big cities, such as Philadelphia and Baltimore. For these reasons, many people want to move to this area. The price of land, in turn, has become very expensive. A farmer may not

be able to afford a nearby farm for his son. So the young farmer might have to move far from his family and friends.

Rising prices for farmland in Lancaster County may drive young Amish couples far from home.

The Outside World

9 Travel isn't easy for the Amish. Going to church or visiting family in a horse and buggy takes time. As more people move to Lancaster, traffic problems get worse. Driving a buggy on crowded roads can be dangerous.

10 To those problems, add the tourists. Every summer, about five million tourists visit Amish country. Traffic becomes a nightmare. Most tourists are there to see the Amish, who have to put up with cars and buses full of people staring at them.

11 Tourism has made life difficult in other ways. The Amish must sometimes listen to unkind comments about their clothes and way of life. They must watch their food, homes, and crafts turned into tourist attractions.

Moving Out

12 Because of these pressures, many Amish families have moved away. Leaving the home settlement is hard. Many have lived their whole lives in one place. Farmhouses might be attached to one another. Grandparents live in one, parents in another, and perhaps a third generation next door. Births, weddings, worship, and funerals

all take place at home. Children go to the same school. Nearby relatives help one another.

13   After family, the church district is most important to the Amish. It includes about 25 to 35 families. It's kept small so that Sunday services can be held in one house. People from the same district try to move together. When moving, they look for a quiet place with good land. As one member said, "Good soil makes a strong church."

The Amish have banned owning cars, which threaten to take members out of the community.

IN THE BUSINESS WORLD

14 For the Amish who stay, there still aren't enough farms. So many Amish have started their own businesses. Some trades, such as blacksmithing, have always existed in the community. Others, such as the roadside vegetable stands, fit in with farming. Still others are aimed at tourists, such as selling quilts and other crafts.

15 The Amish prefer businesses that keep them in their community. Many of their customers are other Amish people. They may not earn as much as they would at outside jobs, but they're with their own people.

16 The Amish are good carpenters. And because the Amish people value hard work,

contractors[5] are eager to hire them. Amish call outsiders "the English." The English contractors pick up the men and drive them to work in cars.

17   Some Amish don't like this contact with the English. It takes men away from their families and communities. And their children don't learn farming. As one saying goes, "The lunch pail is the greatest threat to our way of life."

18   Amish women run businesses, too. That's because the high cost of living demands a second income. Women work as cooks and bakers. And many work together making quilts, which have become very popular.

19   Retired farmers often run a business, such as a general store. The Amish rely on the church when they retire. They don't take Social Security money from the government. So the extra money from a business helps out.

TECHNOLOGY

20 The Amish look at new inventions carefully. One member of the community tries out the invention. The community then decides whether it will be good or bad for them. The

---

[5] contractors: persons who agree to perform work or provide supplies at a certain price or within a certain time

Amish women make patterned quilts, which are always popular with tourists.

decision is based on how the invention will affect their beliefs.

21   In the past, some Amish had electricity. But now it is banned. The Amish think electricity makes people less self-sufficient. They fear it will weaken family life and lead to things like watching television. They also fear that electricity might be used to run machinery that would take jobs away from people.

22   Some Amish farmers used to drive tractors. But tractors are expensive. And many farmers

These young Amish women are on their way to a Sunday "sing" in Lancaster County.

were afraid this would lead to some people owning more land than others. Then they would no longer be equals. They also thought that owning tractors would lead to owning cars. Cars might take people far away from the community.

23   Instead of using these things, the Amish have made their own inventions. They have designed windmills, generators, and other aids to run equipment. They have built farm machinery and equipment to repair the machinery.

WHAT'S AHEAD?

24 Many things threaten the Amish community. They are being pushed off their land by newcomers and high prices. Jobs away from the

farm weaken their traditions. Money threatens their values.

25   One Amish man says, "Families are not as tightly knit as they used to be. No one wants to work seven days a week anymore. But you can't get away from it—they just aren't making any more land, and there's no better place to raise a family than a farm. We must either adapt to Lancaster County's ways or move."

26   Some Amish feel they are being tested. They want to preserve their way of living. If not in Lancaster County, perhaps they will find another place with peace and good farmland. ♦

QUESTIONS

1. Where is the oldest Amish community in America?

2. What is the main kind of work the Amish do?

3. What do the Amish use for transportation?

4. Why do builders like to hire Amish workers?

5. Why do some young Amish couples have to move away?

1   Itzhak [Eet'•tsahk] Perlman is a world-famous violinist from Israel. He also is known as a spokesperson for the disabled.

2   If you asked fellow musicians about Itzhak Perlman, they would likely first mention his cheerful personality. Then they might rave about his musical skills. Last, they might tell you that he is disabled. He cannot walk without the aid of braces and crutches.

ILLNESS STRIKES

3   Perlman's paralysis[1] [puh•ral'•ih•sis] is the result of polio. In 1949, when he was four years old, a polio epidemic[2] hit parts of Israel. Polio vaccines[3] [vak•seens'] were not yet in use. At that time, the treatment for polio called for exercising the patient's limbs in warm water. In time, the boy regained strength in his hands and arms. But his legs never fully recovered.

4   Perlman was a determined child. For endless hours, he practiced walking with heavy braces. After some months, he was able to return to

---

[1] paralysis: complete or partial loss of motion in a part of the body

[2] epidemic: a sudden, fast-spreading outbreak or growth

[3] vaccines: mixtures containing a virus given to prevent a disease

*How did a boy who was seriously disabled
become a world-famous violinist?*

Fiddler with a Smile

Along the coast of Israel, the city of Tel Aviv has a mild climate all year round.

school and rejoin his many friends on the playground. Although he couldn't run as before, Perlman did not feel sorry for himself. And he had something special to keep him busy—music.

A NATURAL GIFT

5   The Perlman family loved music. The sounds of operas and symphonies filled their small apartment in Tel Aviv. So it was natural for Perlman's parents to give their son music lessons. The boy began to study the violin. It

would not only keep him occupied but also serve as physical therapy.

6   At the music academy, Perlman's teachers soon realized the boy had unusual ability. He was only 10 when he gave his first solo performance with a well-known orchestra. Musicians from other countries often came to Israel to perform. When they learned of the new violin prodigy[4] [prah'•dih•jee], many people went to hear Perlman play.

7   At about the same time, a popular television show in the United States was looking for talent. The show's host was Ed Sullivan. Each week's program included a variety of acts. Dancers, comedians, singers, and many other musicians performed. Rudolf Nureyev [Noo•ray'•yuf], Elvis Presley, and Maria Callas were among them.

A Visit to the United States

8 Sullivan had an idea for a show with young performers. On a talent search, he went to a concert in Haifa [High'•fah], Israel. He watched a smiling, stocky boy with crutches come onstage. Sullivan was impressed by the boy's

[4] prodigy: an unusually talented child

performance. He invited Perlman to perform on American television.

9   Ed Sullivan then asked Perlman to join his three-month tour of gifted young musicians. It was called The Ed Sullivan Caravan of Stars. When the tour ended, Perlman and his mother moved to New York City. They decided that New York was now the best place for Perlman to continue his music education. Perlman's father later joined them in the United States.

10   With help from sponsors,[5] Perlman was able to enter Juilliard [Joo'•lee•ard], a world-famous music school. One teacher who auditioned him said, "The development of skill was so far beyond that of any other child, it was just startling. He had large hands, a fluent[6] bowing[7] arm, as well as superb timing and exceptional coordination [koh•or•din•ay'•shun]."

RISING STAR

11   Perlman was on his way to a career as a concert violinist. When he was 17, his teachers felt he was ready to play at Carnegie Hall. He made his

---

[5] sponsors: persons or groups who pay the costs for a project or activity
[6] fluent: done in a smooth, easy way
[7] bowing: playing a stringed instrument with a bow

Perlman was only 13 years old when he appeared on the Ed Sullivan show in 1958.

debut [day•byoo'] on March 5, 1963. The young artist looked forward to the critics' reviews. But because of a newspaper strike, the concert went unreported. News of the violin prodigy got around by word of mouth anyway.

12   In 1964, Perlman entered an important competition. It offered prize money and the chance to appear with major symphony orchestras. Out of 40 applicants, the judges chose 10 semifinalists [seh•mee•fyn'•uhl•ists]. Perlman was the youngest. He won first place playing the music of Mozart [Moh'•tsart],

Tchaikovsky [Chy•kawv'•skee], Bach [Bock], and other famous composers.

13   For the contest, Perlman had borrowed a very rare 200-year-old violin. As people came up to congratulate him afterward, he set the violin aside. When he went to pick it up later, the violin was gone. The next day, it was found in a local pawn shop and quickly returned to Perlman. For only $15, someone had pawned the priceless instrument!

14   Newspapers reported the theft along with rave reviews of Perlman's performance. One critic said: "He is the major talent among the younger generation of fiddlers and the missing link in the great tradition."

15   Perlman's career took off like a meteor. His schedule was soon filled with many live performances, recordings, television shows, and

Perlman rose above his disability to become a world-class violinist of the 20th century. Yet he makes time to speak out for the disabled.

practice. His guest appearances on television have included "60 Minutes," "The Frugal Gourmet" [Goor•may'], and "Sesame Street." Imagine how much fun he had playing the violin for Oscar the Grouch!

Perlman is featured in a concert with fellow fiddler Pinchas Zukerman. The two often perform together.

LIKE EVERYONE ELSE

16 With all his fame, Perlman never forgot about the special problems that people with disabilities face every day. He serves on committees and speaks to groups. He tells them that disabled people want to be treated like everyone else. He speaks out about the lack of handicapped facilities [fuh•sil'•ih•tees] in hotels and public buildings. Perlman's efforts have made building designers more aware of the needs of the disabled.

17   Perlman likes to visit schools and hospitals. He cheers up the children with jokes. His sense of humor carries over to concert audiences, too. Once, during a performance, a string on his violin broke. Instead of going backstage, Perlman stayed on to chat with the audience while he repaired the violin string.

18   Itzhak Perlman ranks high among the outstanding violinists of the 20th century. His playing, as well as his personality, is filled with vigor and joy. His disability could have turned Perlman into an unhappy person. Instead, he faces the world with a smile. ♦

QUESTIONS

1. How old was Itzhak Perlman when he first soloed with a major symphony orchestra?

2. Why do people say Perlman has a cheerful personality?

3. How has Perlman helped the causes of disabled people?

4. How did Perlman come to first perform on national U.S. television?

5. Why was there no newspaper review of Perlman's Carnegie Hall debut?

*In which lands are some of the world's
most beautiful churches? Why were
these huge structures built?*

Stairways

to Heaven

*The windows of Chartres Cathedral in France
are the finest examples of stained-glass artistry
of the Middle Ages.*

1 The Middle Ages—the time in history from about A.D. 500 to A.D. 1500—are known for knights in armor. During this time people believed the sun revolved around Earth. But the later Middle Ages are also known as a period of huge growth in Europe. It was then that building the grand churches of Europe began.

2 In Western Europe, there are more than 100 great cathedrals. Others dot lands throughout the rest of the world. It's amazing that these cathedrals were built at all, let alone built at around the same time. In France, work on six of these great churches began within 80 years of each other.

THE FINEST CHURCH

3 The word *cathedral* means "church of the throne." The seat of the Roman Catholic bishop of an area, a cathedral is most often the finest church in the bishop's district.

4 Inside a cathedral, arches opened into a large space that made people feel swept toward heaven. Using paint, stone, and glass, artists outdid each other creating religious scenes. Nobles and common people alike came to worship there and mark important events in life.

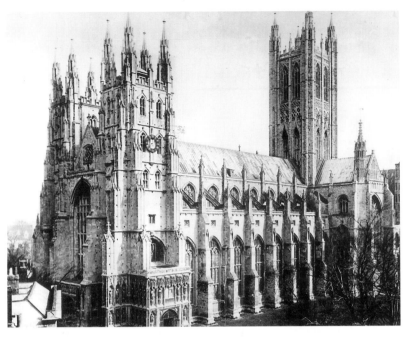

A classic example of Gothic style, England's Canterbury Cathedral became the richest cathedral in Europe.

Years of Building

5   Building a cathedral usually took 40 to 80 years. But some took hundreds of years to finish. People might watch the construction of a cathedral as children, then through their whole lives never see it completed. Fires, lightning, and wars damaged many cathedrals.

6   The construction of such a building changed life for everyone in the town. For years and years, people saw little more than stone walls

and scaffolds.[1] The whole town would be dusty from the construction and from oxen dragging tons of stone to the town from the quarry.[2] Hundreds of strangers came to town for work. Among them were diggers, stonecutters, carpenters, laborers, masons, roofers, painters, and glassworkers.

7   A cathedral was the center of all activity. Because all of Western Europe was Roman Catholic, the whole town was involved in building such a huge church. This important structure was meant not only to glorify religion but to be a credit to the city. Cathedrals were used even before they were finished. A priest famous for his sermons would draw crowds from far and wide. Weddings, funerals, and town meetings all took place in the church. Putting a new stained-glass window or sculpture in place was a big event for the town.

THREE MAIN STYLES

8   Most cathedrals in the Middle Ages were built using three main styles: Byzantine [Biz'•uhn•teen], Romanesque [Roh•muhn•esk'], and

---

[1] scaffolds: elevated platforms built as a support for workers

[2] quarry: an open pit usually for obtaining building stone, slate, or limestone

Richly decorated with marble and mosaics on a golden background, St. Mark's is known as the church of gold.

Gothic [Gahth'•ik]. Some designs blended these styles. Early cathedrals in Italy and France were mostly Byzantine or Romanesque. Some of the later churches in England were Gothic.

9 Byzantine style used round arches and low domes on blocks. Inside the domes are mosaics [moh•zay'•iks]—pictures made of thousands of bits of colored stone—or perhaps paintings. Romanesque style used thick stone walls, towers, round arches, and vaulted[3] ceilings.

10 Gothic style used pointed arches, ribbed vaults, and flying buttresses[4] jutting from outside walls. Although built of stone, Gothic

---

[3] vaulted: arched or domed
[4] flying buttresses: arched structures that extend beyond a wall or building and support it

Gleaming like heavenly jewels, each of Chartres Cathedral's 176 windows tells a story.

buildings are usually tall and slim. They contain fine woodwork, giving them a warmer look than stone. Later still is the Renaissance[5] [Ren'•uh•sahns] style. It used some Gothic forms but newer methods of construction.

---

[5] Renaissance: the period of European history between the 14th and 17th centuries, marked by a fresh interest in art, literature, and science

Both bell towers of the massive Notre Dame Cathedral in Paris, France, are 223 feet high.

Some of the Greats

11 ***St. Mark's Basilica***, Venice, was started in 830 and finished in 1095. The best example of a Byzantine cathedral, the church is shaped like a cross with four arms. A dome covers each arm, with a fifth dome in the middle. Four bronze horses decorate the front door. On the inside walls and under the domes are shining mosaics.

12   Work on ***Notre Dame Cathedral***, Paris, began in 1163 and ended in 1235. This cathedral with two towers is a famous place to visit in France. Its flying buttresses showed off a new style. But Notre Dame is not as grand a

cathedral as that of Chartres [Shart], Reims [Rehmz], and Amiens [Ah•myan'], which followed soon after.

13   ***Canterbury Cathedral***, the "mother church of England," dates to 1175. It was the first cathedral in England to use the French Gothic style. A Norman[6] cathedral had stood on the spot before. In 1170, Thomas Becket was killed there. Soon afterward, he was named a saint. Because of him, the old cathedral drew many visitors from far and near. It became the richest cathedral in Europe.

14   ***Chartres Cathedral*** was built in France in 1194. It took the place of an older cathedral that had burned. This Gothic church is famous for its beautiful stained glass. Every window at ground level has 20 to 30 small pictures in glass. Each tells a story from the Bible or about a saint. People took great care to preserve the stained-glass windows of the cathedral during World War I and World War II. Workers removed the windows at the onset of these wars, then set them back in when the wars ended.

---

[6] Norman: relating to the people of Normandy in northern France who conquered England in 1066

Cologne Cathedral contains relics and art treasures that span thousands of years.

15   ***Reims Cathedral***, also in France, was started in 1210. It was here that the kings of France were crowned. For that reason, it became a target during wars. After being shelled during World War I, the church was rebuilt. Reims Cathedral contains 5,000 statues of bishops, saints, kings, knights, and common people.

16   ***Amiens*** is a great Romanesque cathedral built in France in 1220. Carved in stone are a complete Bible story and a history of the 13th century.

17   ***Cologne*** [Koh•lone'] is the largest Gothic cathedral in northern Europe. It is the pride of Germany, although many call it a "French cathedral on German soil." The grand plan for

it began in 1162. Holy Roman Emperor Frederick I wanted a church to house precious relics. Construction went on for hundreds of years. It stopped in 1560 and didn't start again until 1842. It was finished at last in 1880.

18   ***St. Peter's Basilica*** sits on top of Vatican Hill in Rome, where St. Peter, founder of the Roman Catholic Church, is buried. Like Canterbury, this cathedral was built on the site of an older one. The first St. Peter's was 1,000 years old when it was torn down in 1506. Many were outraged. But work on the new basilica

When the pope makes a speech, people gather in St. Peter's Square to hear him.

Thousands visit St. Peter's Basilica, which contains Michelangelo's famous sculpture, the Pietà [Pee•ay•tah'].

went on through several starts and stops. In 1546, the pope hired Michelangelo [Mee•kel•ahn'•jay•loh], at age 71, to help finish it. Michelangelo designed the main dome but died before everything was done. The pope lives beside the cathedral and celebrates important days there.

19   **St. Basil's**, Moscow, is unlike the cathedrals in Europe because it has no large open space inside. It is one of the most interesting churches in the world. An eight-sided dome covers the main chapel, which has eight other chapels around it. Each of these is capped by a colorful onion-shaped dome. St. Basil's was built in the late 1500s by orders of Ivan IV, better known

as Ivan the Terrible. Although it is not of true Byzantine style, St. Basil's has a Byzantine look.

20   These short descriptions give but a few details of the great cathedrals. There are many more of these grand structures throughout the world. Fine cathedrals have been built in recent times as well. You may already have visited some or plan to do so one day. As you step back and look at them, perhaps you can trace their shapes back to the great monuments of the Middle Ages. ♦

Questions

1. During which period in history were many of the great cathedrals started?

2. What does the word *cathedral* mean?

3. How long did it usually take to build a cathedral?

4. What are the three main building styles of a cathedral?

*How did a Chicago stabbing victim
help solve her own murder?*

CAN THE

DEAD TALK?

1   If you are like most people, you have dreams. Perhaps you have dreamed about a relative who is no longer alive. In your dreams, that person may have spoken in a normal manner. Still, you knew they were only dreams. Some people, though, believe that the dead can communicate[1] with the living.

---

[1] communicate: make contact with

The Séance

2   In the early 1900s, many people were caught up in the séance [say'•ahntz] craze. In a typical séance, a small group of people gathered at a table around a medium. The medium was a messenger between the living and those on "the other side." Séances were usually held in a darkened room, which set an eerie [eer'•ee] mood. The medium might appear to be in a trance, or semiconscious[2] state, as he or she received messages. Most séances were later proved to be hoaxes.[3]

Modern Medium

3   Over the years, the popularity of séances died down. But in the past 20 years, there has been renewed interest in hearing from those who have passed on. One modern-day medium is George Anderson. He doesn't sit in darkened rooms or go into a trance. Instead, he has appeared on radio and television, where thousands of people can hear him.

4   The mother of a young man who was killed in an accident contacted Anderson. She heard of his work in communicating with the

---

[2] semiconscious: not fully alert or active
[3] hoaxes: acts intended to trick or mislead

By using some of the objects surrounding him, this diviner claims to contact spirits of the dead.

dead. The woman had a feeling that her son wanted to "talk" to her. Anderson agreed to see her. They both decided that a private meeting would be better than one broadcast publicly. This was due to a police case that was pending[4] on the accident. Anderson did allow her husband and others to be present.

5   Anderson explained that once he made contact with the son, he would ask the mother questions. He expected only short replies, mostly yes or no. As he made contact with the son, Anderson brought forth many of the son's

---

[4] pending: not yet decided or acted on

Some spiritualists of today use special objects like magic bottles, water, and various images.

thoughts. The son "asked" about members of the family. He also "told" of meeting friends and relatives who had died before him. The son related that he was not angry about the accident and that he felt at peace.

UNFINISHED BUSINESS

6 Another account of contact with the dead also has to do with sudden death. In 1977, a woman in Chicago died from stab wounds. Not long after the tragedy, a co-worker reported that her deceased friend had spoken to her about the

murder. The co-worker was then able to name the killer, who worked at the same hospital as the two women.

7   In 1987, a tragic airplane accident occurred in Indianapolis. A jet rammed into a motel. Some of the victims worked at the motel. The mother of a young man who worked at the front desk got word of the crash. She received a call from someone who had heard a report over the radio. When she hung up the phone, it rang again. This time it was her son calling. He told her he was fine. However, later at the accident scene, she learned that her son had indeed been killed by the falling aircraft.

Visitors to this spiritualist camp in the Midwest try to reach loved ones who have died.

The Lincolns (left) and Thomas Edison (right) were among many famous people who sought to make contact with the dead.

PAST BELIEVERS

8 Claims of talking with the dead aren't new. In fact, some famous people of the past were believers. President Abraham Lincoln and his wife, Mary Todd Lincoln, held séances in the White House. Their son Willie had died of typhoid[5] at the age of 12. Mrs. Lincoln hired a medium so they might communicate with Willie. That may be one reason some people considered Mrs. Lincoln odd.

---

[5] typhoid: a disease that causes fever, weakness, and diarrhea and is passed from one person to another in dirty food or water

9   Nor did Thomas Alva Edison, the famous inventor, keep his beliefs a secret. He spoke about the possibility of the dead contacting the living. Edison, in fact, was working to invent a new machine that might accomplish this communication. Unfortunately, he died before completing the project.

10   We'll never know what marvelous invention Edison might have produced. Of course, another genius may one day take up the cause of letting the departed speak for themselves. ♦

QUESTIONS

1. Why did George Anderson and his client decide on a private meeting instead of a public broadcast?

2. How was a typical séance conducted?

3. Why did President and Mrs. Lincoln hold séances in the White House?

*Why is soccer the most popular
game in the world?*

THE TRUE WORLD CHAMPIONSHIP

1 See if you already know these facts about soccer: Eleven players are on each team. They score by moving a ball past the other team's goal line. Thousands of fans show up to watch the games. Soccer's greatest star ever was Pelé.

2 Perhaps the first three statements may remind you of American-style football. But they also describe soccer. In fact, in many countries the game of soccer is called association [uhs• so•see• ay'•shun] football.

SOCCER'S HISTORY

3 Soccer is a very old game. Some people think that the ancient Romans played an early kind of soccer. Roman soldiers took their game all over Europe. Over time, the game spread to other continents.

Germany's Stefan Effenberg takes a tumble into the goal during a 1994 World Cup game played in Chicago.

After many years, the game adopted the rules it follows today.

4   The most important rule has to do with touching the ball. At no time may players—except goalkeepers—touch the ball with their hands. Players use their feet, heads, and bodies. For example, they might stop a ball with their chest. They may kick a ball coming at them toward a teammate. Or players might kick the

ball straight up. As the ball falls, players can use their head to push it forward.

5   Another rule has to do with substitutes.[1] No more than three are allowed. Sometimes a team uses up all three substitutes and then loses a player. Perhaps someone is injured or thrown out by the referee. That team must then continue with only 10 players.

---

[1] substitutes: players who take the place of other players

6   In soccer, there are no time-outs. The only break comes between the two 45-minute halves. So players must run throughout each half.

The Playing Field

7 A soccer playing field is a rectangle. For a league[2] game, the rectangle is 100 to 130 yards (90 to 119 meters) long. It's between 50 and 100 yards (46 and 90 meters) wide. A halfway line is drawn across the middle of the field. At each end is a goal area—eight yards (7.3 meters) wide and eight feet (2.4 meters) high. The field also has markings to show corners, penalty areas around the goal areas, and the center circle.

8   Play begins with a coin toss. The losing team chooses the side of the field it will protect. Then each team lines up its players. The goalkeeper stays near the goal. Two fullbacks stand before the goalkeeper. Three halfbacks stand before the fullbacks. Five forwards stand between them and the other team.

9   The team that won the coin toss kicks off. Its kicker goes into the center circle and boots the ball into the other team's area. After that, both teams struggle for the ball and for goals. A

---

[2] league: persons or groups united for common interests or goals

Endurance, teamwork, and good game planning are important skills in soccer.

referee and two linesmen make sure everybody follows the rules.

10   Teamwork is very important. Remember, there are no time-outs for huddles and coaching. So every player must know what to expect from teammates. Teams have their own styles. Some like to move the ball forward in short passes. Others go for powerful, long kicks.

MODERN SOCCER

11 Modern soccer began in England in 1863. That year the Football Association was created and rules were set up. By 1885, England had

Largely because of Pelé, soccer became popular in the United States.

professional teams. Teams quickly formed in other countries. In 1904, FIFA (Fédération Internationale de Football Association), an international group, was formed to control the sport. By 1994, 190 countries had joined FIFA.

12   Since 1900, almost every Summer Olympics has included soccer games. But from the first, few countries sent teams. All their best players were professionals, or "pros," and pros were not allowed to play. Fans wanted to see the pros compete in international matches. So, in 1930, FIFA started an international pro tournament.[3]

13   Known as the World Cup, this tournament takes place every four years. It is the most-watched sporting event in the world. The World Cup draws a television audience of more than a

---

[3] tournament: a contest or series of contests played for a championship

billion people. Each country's all-stars form its national team. They play in many qualifying[4] rounds. Finally, the top teams meet from around the world. The World Cup of 1994 was held in the United States. The top 24 teams played 31 games over 52 days.

14   The U.S. team was one of the 24 finalists in the 1994 World Cup. However, soccer isn't as popular in the United States as football, basketball, or baseball. Why, then, was the '94 World Cup held in the United States? FIFA members believe that U.S. fans can be won over to soccer. As proof, they point to the crowds who came to the U.S. pro soccer games from 1975 to 1977. During those years, the superstar Pelé played for the New York Cosmos.

15   Pelé had become a world-famous player. He helped Brazil's national teams win three World Cups—in 1958, 1962, and 1970. No other country had won it three times!*

THE GREATEST PLAYER

16 Pelé was born in Brazil in 1940. His father was a soccer player, so Pelé grew up with the game. When he was 16, he won a place with the

*Brazil won the 1994 World Cup.

---

[4] qualifying: limiting or narrowing down

Pelé played a 1990 exhibition game in Milan, Italy, to celebrate his 50th birthday.

major-league Santos club. The next year he played on the national team. His stunning play in the 1958 tournament brought Brazil its first World Cup. For most of the next 17 years, Brazil's national team was the greatest in World Cup soccer.

17 Pelé isn't a large man, but he was strong and quick. He played for a long time without tiring. In a fast-moving game, he could plan several steps ahead. His eyesight was so good that he could react before others even saw the ball. Pelé became a national hero in his teens.

18   In 1977, Pelé decided to retire from Brazilian soccer. But he heard about a new pro league in the United States. So he came to join the Cosmos. Pelé thrilled the crowds who came to see him play what he had called "the beautiful game." Since then, interest in soccer has remained higher than ever before.

19   Fifteen years after Pelé retired, an unusual election was held. Nearly a thousand voters around the world picked an all-time World Cup team. Pelé's name showed up on every ballot. At the 1994 World Cup games, both fans and players were thrilled to get his autograph. Pelé is still the most important person in the history of soccer. ♦

QUESTIONS

1. How many players has each soccer team?

2. What is the rule about touching the ball?

3. In what country did modern soccer have its start?

4. What is the World Cup?

5. Who is the most famous soccer player?

A MAN WITH A VISION

1   Luís Muñoz Marín believed in his native land, Puerto Rico. He loved the people and worked hard for their welfare. Because of him, Puerto Ricans of his era and beyond could look to a brighter future.

AN IMPORTANT YEAR

2   Luís Muñoz Marín was born in 1898 in Puerto Rico, a small island south of Florida. It was an important year. Spain had sunk the U.S. battleship *Maine* in Havana Harbor. In April of that year, the United States declared war on Spain. Four months later, the United States won the Spanish-American War. Under the Treaty of

Can one person make a difference?
What is special about a man
who put his country first?

Muñoz's hard work to get jobs and farmland for Puerto Ricans greatly improved life there.

Paris, the territories of Guam [Gwahm], Puerto Rico, and the Philippines would all be under U.S. rule.

3   Now Puerto Rico was no longer owned by Spain but by the United States. Either way, the people of Puerto Rico weren't happy. They wanted more control over their own land.

A Famous Father

4   Muñoz's father was Luís Muñoz Rivera.[1] He was a powerful man in Puerto Rico. Before the war, he had talked Spain into giving Puerto Ricans more freedom. After the war, he asked the United States for the same rights. In 1910, the Puerto Rican people sent Muñoz Rivera to the U.S. Congress in Washington, D.C. He argued against a law that denied Puerto Ricans the right to elect their own government officials. Instead, they were appointed by the U.S. president. Although Muñoz Rivera worked hard to change the law, he died before it was finally changed. But his strong love for his country had a lasting effect on his son.

---

[1] Luís Muñoz Rivera: In Spanish-speaking countries, people have two last names. The first is the family name of the father, such as Muñoz. The second is the family name of the mother, such as Rivera or Marín.

Once a fortress and now the governor's mansion, La Fortaleza graces the old section of Puerto Rico's capital, San Juan.

5   Luís Muñoz Marín had moved to Washington with his father. He went to high school and college there. Later he tried to study law, but his heart was not in it. So, after his father died, Muñoz moved to New York City and became a writer.

A Well-Known Writer

6 Muñoz wrote about the troubles in his homeland. He became well known as a writer in the United States, but he couldn't forget the problems of Puerto Rico. He remembered the hunger and the bad housing. He worried about the lack of jobs and people without hope. Muñoz felt he could make a difference if he went back home.

7 Muñoz returned to Puerto Rico in 1926. He became editor of *La Democracía* [Lah Day•moh krah•see'•ia], the newspaper his father had started. In it, he wrote about the poor living conditions in Puerto Rico and blamed the people in power. He demanded independence from the United States.

In the Senate

8 In 1932, Muñoz was elected to the Puerto Rican Senate.[2] He could speak both Spanish and English, so he was well able to argue Puerto Rico's point of view to people in the United States. President Franklin D. Roosevelt listened to what he had to say. The words of Muñoz began to make a difference.

---

[2] senate: the higher branch of a law-making body of a nation, state, or province

9   However, hard times were coming. During the Depression,[3] businesses worldwide were in trouble. Puerto Rico became even poorer than before. The United States had too many problems of its own to help the small island. Puerto Rican schools became poorer, medicine was hard to get, and jobs were scarce.

10   Muñoz began to change his mind about independence for Puerto Rico. Although it would be good to be independent of the United States, making life better for Puerto Ricans was more important. Muñoz wanted to show the people that his ideas had changed. So he left his political party and began a new one, the Popular Democratic Party. Its purpose was to improve the life of the Puerto Rican people.

11   Muñoz didn't have much money. Even so, he worked hard to take his message to the people. For two years, he visited all areas of Puerto Rico. He spoke to people living in city slums. He talked to farmers in the mountains. He told them that they must help themselves. If they elected his party, he would show them

---

[3] Depression: a period of very low business activity and loss of money worldwide brought on by the stock market crash of 1929

ways to improve their lives. His cry was "Bread! Land! Liberty!"

HEAD OF THE SENATE

12 Muñoz told people not to trust him without question. Instead, he asked them to elect him

Puerto Rico has many beautiful old buildings from the 16th and 17th centuries.

and then watch him carefully. If he didn't keep his promises, they could vote him out of office. The people believed in him, remembering how his father had served the country. In 1940, they voted for his Popular Democratic Party. Muñoz became the president of the Senate.

13   In that office, Muñoz helped small farmers get more land. He worked with the governor, an official chosen by the president of the United States. Soon, many more Puerto Ricans held important jobs in their own land.

14   In 1944, the Popular Democratic Party won the election again. This victory showed that Puerto Ricans trusted Muñoz to carry out his promises. Muñoz knew Puerto Rico needed still more help. He started Operation Bootstrap, a program that brought new businesses to the island and gave jobs to even more people. Life started to improve for Puerto Ricans.

FIRST ELECTED GOVERNOR

15 Then, in 1948, the United States decided to let Puerto Rico elect its own governor. Muñoz won the race in a landslide[4] victory, becoming the first elected governor of Puerto Rico.

---

[4] landslide: a huge victory, especially in a political race

President John F. Kennedy awarded Muñoz the Presidential Medal of Freedom in 1963.

16   Muñoz held the job of governor for 16 years. During that time, many factories were built and businesses started. Muñoz's dream of a better way of life for Puerto Rico was coming true. In 1963, he received the Presidential Medal of Freedom from President John F. Kennedy.

17   In 1964, Muñoz decided not to run for governor again. His bewildered friends couldn't understand why he would want to step down.

Muñoz explained that one person should not be in power for too long. For the good of Puerto Rico, someone else should have a chance to be governor.

18   Muñoz always believed he could make a difference. He dedicated himself to improving life in Puerto Rico. He began with little money and almost no power. But he became one of the most famous, respected, and beloved men of his time. ♦

QUESTIONS

1. When and where was Luís Muñoz Marín born?

2. Why did Muñoz attend school in Washington, D.C.?

3. Why did Muñoz decide to return to Puerto Rico?

4. What offices did Muñoz hold?

5. Why did Muñoz step down from office at the peak of his career?

*Why was there no October 5
in the year 1582?*

The Difference a Day Makes

1 Monday, Tuesday, Wednesday, Thursday. . . .
Days, weeks, and months are organized on the
calendar. It looks so natural, as if things have
always been this way. But they haven't. It took
a long, long time to arrive at the system we call
the modern calendar.

2 You could think of our calendar as the fight
to get the sun and moon together. This struggle
has gone on for thousands of years. And it
hasn't been won yet!

BROTHER SUN, SISTER MOON

3 In the earliest days, people had no calendar.
There was no true way of counting time. People
saw that the sun came up and went down, over

*Without a good way to count time, it was hard
for people to know when to plant crops.*

Symbols of nature represent winter,
spring, summer, and fall.

and over. Sometimes they kept a record of this by making a notch on a stick. Or they knotted a cord. Calling the span of time from sun to sun a day seemed like a good way to count time.

4   Primitive[1] people also watched the seasons change. Summer came, then winter, then summer again. People tried to keep track of each year. But the length of time in a whole year was very long. People wanted to keep track of

[1] primitive: relating to the earliest age or period

the days and seasons. In this way, they would know when to plant crops. They would know when to get ready for winter. People needed to divide a year's time into shorter pieces. They watched the moon change night after night. They began to measure time by the cycles of the moon. They called this span of time a month.

5   Deciding how many months should make up a year was one problem. The moon goes through its phases in 29½ days. Let's say a month is 29½ days long. At this length, 12 months will produce a year of 354 days. Thirteen months make a year 383½ days long.

6   Today we know that a year is really 365 days, 5 hours, 48 minutes, and 46 seconds long.

Using a 12-year cycle, the Chinese calendar gives each year the name of an animal.

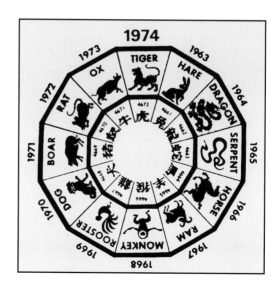

England's ancient Stonehenge monument is thought to have been a kind of calendar.

But centuries ago, people had to try different calendars to find out that months just don't fit neatly into the year. The struggle to create the modern calendar went on for 3,000 years.

EARLY CALENDARS

7 The Babylonian [Bab•ih•loh'•nee•en] calendar switched back and forth between 29-day months and 30-day months. This took care of the half day. But the year was only 354 days long. As time passed, the calendar no longer fit the seasons. So about every four years, the people would add in an extra month. It didn't work very well.

8   The Egyptian calendar years had 365 days. The people divided the year into 12 months. Each month was 30 days long. At the end of the

year, there were five extra days. Nor did the Egyptians do anything about the extra 5 hours and 48 minutes. This time added up, and over the years it threw the calendar off. When the calendar said it was the first day of spring during the dead of winter, there were problems.

9   The Roman calendar was even less reliable[2] than the Egyptian one. The Roman calendar had 10 months, beginning with Martius [Mar'•tee• uhs], or March. The year was only 304 days long. The 60 days left over fell during winter. People simply skipped this block of time by not including these days on the calendar!

10   The Romans did, however, leave us their names for the months of the year. You can see that the winter months of January and February are missing from the following list: Martius [Mar'•tee•uhs], Aprilis [Ay•pril'•is], Maius [My'•uhs], Junius [Joo'•nee•uhs], Quintilis [Kwin•til'•ihs] (now called July), Sextilis [Sex• til'•ihs] (now called August), September, October, November, and December.

11   One Roman king thought that the 60 winter days were too important to leave out. During that time, he couldn't collect taxes. So he added

---

[2] reliable: fit to be trusted

the months of Januarius [Jan•yoo•air'•ee•uhs] and Februarius [Feb•roo•air'•ee•uhs] to the end of the year.

THE JULIAN CALENDAR

12 In 46 B.C. (46 years before the birth of Christ), Julius Caesar ruled Rome. By then, the Roman calendar was off not by two but by three months! Caesar told the Romans to give up using the moon to count the months. He, too, divided the year into 12 months. Like the Babylonians, he changed the number of days in a month. Each one would be 30 or 31 days long. February would have 29 days. But Caesar made every fourth year a leap year. This meant that,

Julius Caesar (left) matched the new calendar to the seasons. Pope Gregory XIII (right) added the finishing touches.

in such a year, February would have an extra day, or 30 days. This system took in the extra quarter day (5 hours and 48 minutes). Caesar also moved the New Year to January 1st.

13   Now the task was to make the new calendar fit the seasons. Caesar made the year 46 B.C. 445 days long. The Romans called it the "year of confusion." But the new calendar worked much better than earlier ones. To honor the king, the Romans changed the name of the month of Quintilis. They named it after Julius Caesar, and we call it *July*.

EQUAL TIME

14 The next ruler, Emperor Augustus, wanted a month named after *him* as well. So Sextilis was called Augustus. An old story tells how Augustus took one more day away from February. He added it to August to make it 31 days. The new emperor wanted his month to be just as long as July, the month of Julius Caesar.

15   This calendar worked even better. But it still wasn't perfect. The calendar year was 11 minutes and 14 seconds longer than the sun's year. In time, even these few minutes became a problem. By 1580, the first day of spring was falling on March 11th, 10 days too early.

The Gregorian Calendar

16 In 1582, Pope Gregory XIII (the 13th) was the leader of the Roman Catholic Church. He gave an order to drop 10 days from the current year. He said that the day after October 4 should be October 15. The pope also said that there should be no leap year at the end of a century. But the rule did not hold if the year could be divided evenly by 400. So there was no leap year in 1700, 1800, or 1900. But the year 2000 *is* a leap year.

All Together Now

17 All of the Roman Catholic countries obeyed the pope. They took up the new calendar in 1582. Other countries waited longer. England didn't change to the new calendar until 1752. Russia

The Aztecs of Mexico developed a calendar to fix the time of monthly festivals.

didn't follow until as late as 1918. Until that time, the Russian calendar was more than 10 days off from the rest of the world. And several very old calendar systems are still in use. Three of the most noteworthy are the Jewish, Muslim, and Chinese calendars.

18   Using Pope Gregory's calendar, the year is only 26.3 seconds off from the sun's year. It will take a long, long time before these few seconds amount to a problem. That is, we'll stay on track as long as we remember which year is leap year. ♦

QUESTIONS

1. Which calendar added a month every four years?

2. Which calendar left us names for the months of the year?

3. Who ordered no leap year at the end of a century unless the year could be divided evenly by 400?

4. How did the month of July get its name?

Can a company make a lot of money and do good at the same time?

A New Kind of Company

On the outside wall of their gas station-turned-scoop shop, Ben and Jerry showed movies at a free film festival.

1 Chocolate Chip Cookie Dough ice cream. Blueberry Cheesecake frozen yogurt. New York Super Fudge Chunk ice cream. Peace Pops. Do these names make you want to run to your freezer? If so, you are not alone. These flavors

are creations by Ben & Jerry's Homemade, Inc., one of America's most popular ice cream brands.

2   Ben is Ben Cohen. Jerry is Jerry Greenfield. They both grew up on Long Island in New York. Their friendship began in seventh-grade gym class in 1963.

HOW THEY STARTED

3 As adults, both men were unhappy with the work they were doing. As Jerry says, "We wanted to do something that would be more fun." They also wanted to live in a small town.

4   In 1977, Ben and Jerry moved to Vermont. For $5, they enrolled in a Pennsylvania State University correspondence course[1] on making ice cream. The next year, they renovated[2] a gas station in Burlington, Vermont, and sold ice cream by the scoop. They invested $8,000 of their own money and borrowed $4,000 to start the business.

5   In 1980, they rented space in an old mill where they packed pints of their ice cream. Ben drove his old VW wagon to restaurants and grocery stores in the area selling ice cream.

---

[1] correspondence course: a course of study taken by mail
[2] renovated: made like new again

Ben & Jerry's Traveling Show is just one example of how the pair realized their dream: to improve the world and have fun doing it.

6　　This business was so successful that it expanded. They also moved their scoop shop. And in 1982, their first scoop franchise[3] [fran'•chyz] opened in Vermont.

7　　In 1983, stores in Boston, Massachusetts, began to sell Ben & Jerry's ice cream in pints. But in 1984, Häagen-Dazs, a very big ice cream company owned by Pillsbury, tried to stop the sales. Ben & Jerry's sued them. Three years later, Häagen-Dazs was still trying to stop the sale of Ben & Jerry's ice cream in other states.

---

[3] franchise: the right to sell a company's goods or services in a certain area

Shared Success

8   Ben and Jerry belonged to the "hippie" generation of the late 1960s and early 1970s. Like many people of that time, they questioned the establishment.[4] They wanted to change and improve the world.

9   Ben and Jerry didn't set out to build a big company. But by 1984, the business was growing quickly. They considered selling it because they didn't like big business. They thought it took unfair advantage of workers and the community.

10   They decided not to sell the company. But the pair worked hard to make a company they would be proud to own. They would not use up the workers, the community, or the environment to build their business. Instead, they would share their success.

11   The idea of sharing success is used by many companies today. It means that, as a company succeeds, all the people it touches succeed, too. Employees, customers, suppliers, stockholders, the local, national, as well as international communities are all part of its success.

---

[4] establishment: the social, economic, and political leaders who form the ruling class of a nation

Quality Product

12 Vermont is a poor state. It has many small farms that raise cows for milk. From the start, Ben and Jerry decided they would use milk and cream only from Vermont to make their ice cream. When the U.S. government lowered the price of milk, Ben & Jerry's kept right on paying the higher price.

13   Ben & Jerry's has a goal for its products. It is "To make, distribute, and sell the finest quality, all-natural ice cream and related products in a wide variety of innovative[5] flavors made from Vermont dairy products."

Good Causes

14 In 1985, Ben and Jerry gave money to start a foundation.[6] The foundation gets 7.5 percent of the company's profits before taxes. The foundation gives money to help causes Ben & Jerry's believes in. These causes mostly serve communities, poor people, the environment, and children. Ben & Jerry's also gives away lots of ice cream to schools and charities.

---

[5] innovative: new

[6] foundation: an organization supported by ongoing contributions

15   Improving local communities is important to Ben & Jerry's. In Vermont, the company supports banks that provide low-cost loans to farms and small businesses. It supports a charity that builds homes that people can afford to buy. In the South, the company works with the Federation of Southern Cooperatives. It helps to preserve small farms owned by black families. This is where Ben & Jerry's buys its pecans.

16   The company also sets up partnerships with charities. One scoop shop in the Harlem section of New York is a training ground for homeless people. Its profits go to a shelter. In Baltimore, Maryland, another scoop shop is run by the disabled. Yet another in Vermont is staffed by at-risk children.

A Fair Shake

17 Ben & Jerry's thinks about its employees, too. In a poor state, it pays them well. It offers generous benefits. It has a bonus plan based on the company's profits. The size of the bonus does not depend on how high up an employee is. Instead, the bonus is based on how long he or she has worked for the company.

18   From the start, Ben and Jerry had another unusual idea. The highest-paid employee could

not earn more than five times the salary of the lowest-paid employee. With the growth of the company, this has changed. But Ben & Jerry's still sees to it that there is not too big a difference between the top and bottom salaries.

THE ENVIRONMENT

19 Ben & Jerry's also works hard to protect the environment. The company tries to save energy and control waste. One way it controls some waste is through recycling. Ice cream that is spilled is sent to a farm. There, it is fed to the pigs. Ben & Jerry's reports that the pigs' favorite flavor is Cherry Garcia. The animals would not eat Mint Chocolate Cookie.

20 Ben & Jerry's also plants trees to replace those used in making the wooden sticks inside Peace Pops, its chocolate-coated ice cream bars. The company is looking for a product to take the place of sticks. The sale of Ben & Jerry's Rainforest Crunch ice cream helps preserve the world's rain forests. Nuts in the ice cream come from rain forest trees.

SPREADING THE JOY

21 A sense of fun is also important at Ben & Jerry's. It has sent "Cowmobiles" (mobile homes)

More than a million visitors have toured Ben & Jerry's Waterbury, Vermont, plant to see how ice cream is made.

across the country handing out ice cream. It has also sent the Ben & Jerry's New Vaudeville[7] Light Circus Bus around the country. The bus features street jugglers and magicians and gives away ice cream as well. The bus has panels on top of it that use energy from the sun to power the electronic equipment on board. The bus is a fun way to encourage people to use solar energy if they can. Ben & Jerry's also sponsors folk music festivals. And Ben & Jerry's is one of the most popular tourist places in Vermont. Visitors to the plant see how ice cream is made and enjoy other attractions there.

22   Not everything is perfect at Ben & Jerry's. But everyone there is working to make the

---

[7] vaudeville: a kind of theatrical show of the past made up of a variety of songs, dances, and comic acts

Pictured are Ben and Jerry, founders of an ice cream empire.

company even better. Employees take pride in their work and feel good about their company. More people want to work there than there are jobs available.

23   Today, Ben and Jerry and their families live near the company in Vermont. Ben & Jerry's is a big, successful company that is also able to do good. You might say that the friends have found a way to have their ice cream cake and eat it, too! ♦

QUESTIONS

1. Why did Ben and Jerry want to start a business?

2. Why did they think of selling the business when it was growing so quickly?

3. List some of the worthy causes adopted by Ben & Jerry's.

4. On what is Ben & Jerry's company bonus plan based?

5. How does the company work to protect the environment?

GLOSSARY

SETTING THE SKY ON FIRE
Pages 4–13
muskets: heavy guns used before modern rifles

FAITH, FAMILY, AND FARMING
Pages 14–25
ancestors: relatives more distant than grandparents
contractors: persons who agree to perform work or provide supplies at a certain price or within a certain time
persecution: the act of causing someone to suffer because of belief
sects: religious groups having beliefs that differ greatly from those of the main body
self-sufficient: able to take care of oneself without outside help

FIDDLER WITH A SMILE
Pages 26–35
bowing: playing a stringed instrument with a bow
epidemic: a sudden, fast-spreading outbreak or growth
fluent: done in a smooth, easy way
paralysis: complete or partial loss of motion in a part of the body
prodigy: an unusually talented child
sponsors: persons or groups who pay the costs for a project or activity
vaccines: mixtures containing a virus given to prevent a disease

STAIRWAYS TO HEAVEN
Pages 36–47
flying buttresses: arched structures that extend beyond a wall or building and support it
Norman: relating to the people of Normandy in northern France who conquered England in 1066
quarry: an open pit usually for obtaining building stone, slate, or limestone
Renaissance: the period of European history between the 14th and 17th centuries, marked by a fresh interest in art, literature, and science
scaffolds: elevated platforms built as a support for workers
vaulted: arched or domed

CAN THE DEAD TALK?
Pages 48–55
communicate: make contact with
hoaxes: acts intended to trick or mislead
pending: not yet decided or acted on
semiconscious: not fully alert or active
typhoid: a disease that causes fever, weakness, and diarrhea and is passed from one person to another in dirty food or water

THE TRUE WORLD CHAMPIONSHIP
Pages 56–65
league: persons or groups united for common interests or goals
qualifying: limiting or narrowing down
substitutes: players who take the place of other players
tournament: a contest or series of contests played for a championship

A MAN WITH A VISION
Pages 66–75
Depression: the period of very low business activity and loss of money worldwide brought on by the stock market crash of 1929
landslide: a huge victory, especially in a political race
senate: the higher branch of a law-making body of a nation, state, or province

THE DIFFERENCE A DAY MAKES
Pages 76–85
primitive: relating to the earliest age or period
reliable: fit to be trusted

A NEW KIND OF COMPANY
Pages 86–94
correspondence course: a course of study taken by mail
establishment: the social, economic, and political leaders who form the ruling class of a nation
foundation: an organization supported by ongoing contributions
franchise: the right to sell a company's goods or services in a certain area
innovative: new
renovated: made like new again
vaudeville: a kind of theatrical show of the past made up of a variety of songs, dances, and comic acts

THE CONTEMPORARY READER
VOLUME 1, NUMBERS 1-6

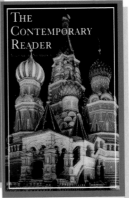

The Contemporary Readers offer nonfiction stories—intriguing, inspiring, and thought provoking—that address current adult issues and interests through lively writing and colorful photography.